MW00915150

God's Remnant

When God

Awakens You

WORKBOOK

Jan F. Solvberg
Palma Korosi

JF Velkey-
Sølvberg
PUBLISHING

CONTENTS

INTRODUCTION

Welcome to an enlightening journey of discovery and understanding with God's Remnant – When God. This thought-provoking workbook is designed to guide you through the hidden truths of God's Remnant, offering a unique opportunity to engage in personal or group study.

This workbook is inspired by the book, God's Remnant – When God... Awakens you to resurrect the Gospel (tap link or scan to find.)

The book aims to deepen your understanding of important events and issues. It is a tool designed to spark meaningful conversations and align your beliefs with the mysteries uncovered by Pastor Dave.

With 14 chapters to explore, this workbook is ideally suited for a 14-week small group study. Each chapter provides a new opportunity to delve deeper into the teachings of God's Remnant – When God.

Embark on a journey of discovery and understanding with God's Remnant – When God. Welcome aboard!

NIGHTMARE

I will both lie down in peace, and sleep;
For You alone, O LORD,
make me dwell in safety.

— PSALM 4:8

Have you ever experienced an intense wave of guilt that seemed to engulf every aspect of your life? How did you find relief and redemption amidst the overwhelming burden of guilt?

Have you experienced feelings of judgment and condemnation? What triggered these emotions?

How did you navigate through these difficult feelings and find a path to resolution?

Did you rely on support from others, or did you find solace through personal reflection?

How does the depiction of Jesus' appearance strike you?

· · ·

If you encountered Jesus in person, what emotions would you experience?

_____

_____

_____

_____

If you encountered Jesus today, what would your heart's cry be? Would "HELP" be your immediate call, or is there something else you'd express?

_____

_____

_____

_____

Have you encountered someone experiencing an unusual dream lately? Any intriguing dream encounters of your own? What peculiar scenarios unfolded?

_____

_____

_____

_____

Have you aided someone facing a significant health challenge? What did you do in assisting the individual?

_____

_____

_____

_____

Have you ever found yourself in a situation requiring an ambulance? Share the resolution of your ambulance story.

_____

_____

_____

_____

Have you ever accompanied someone to the hospital during the late hours? How did you manage the situation?

_____

_____

_____

_____

Consider Einstein's quote, "Sitting with a pretty girl for an hour seems but a minute; sitting on a hot stove for a minute seems an hour," reflect human perception of time?

Do you agree that time feels different in various situations?

_____

_____

_____

_____

Have you experienced being taken to the hospital during nighttime? Did you find the experience painful or uncomfortable?

_____

_____

_____

_____

Have you ever struggled to fall asleep because of persistent racing thoughts? How do you manage to calm your mind before bedtime?

_____

_____

_____

Who holds the title of your longest-standing confidant? Can you freely discuss any subject, including sensitive or awkward matters, with your trusted friend?

_____

_____

_____

_____

Have you taken a month-long sick leave from work or study? How did your friends, family, and colleagues react to your situation?

_____

_____

_____

_____

Did your absence necessitate finding a substitute? If so, how did they manage?

_____

_____

_____

_____

Reflect on your journey towards recovery during the sick leave period. How did you re-adjust to work or study after such an extended absence?

_____

_____

_____

_____

What do you think of Harry's concern of youngsters dedicating excessive time to computer games and its value in preparation for adulthood?

_____

_____

_____

_____

Do you agree with Harry's claim that engaging in war-themed videogames, can foster dis-respect for weaponry and human life?

_____

_____

_____

_____

What's your opinion on various Christian denominations praying together, despite theological differences?

_____

_____

_____

_____

Have you encountered clashes between Christian doctrines? What were the core issues that led to doctrinal disagreements. How did the conflicts ultimately conclude?

_____

_____

_____

Have you ever needed to recount an unusual anecdote from your life to an audience?

_____

_____

_____

_____

How did the audience react to your story? Were they intrigued, surprised, or perhaps bewildered by the narrative you shared? Were you nervous, excited, or apprehensive about how it would be received?

_____

_____

_____

Have you encountered strangers offering prayer? How did you react? Describe your response to their gesture. What happened after the stranger offered to pray for you?

_____

_____

_____

2
AWAKENING

Therefore He says:
"Awake, you who sleep,
Arise from the dead,
And Christ will give you light."

— EPHESIANS 5:14

Pastor Dave's morning routine is described in this chapter. Does his routine seem unusual to you? What does your typical morning routine look like?

_____

_____

_____

What do you think of this; a pastor seeking insights from a gardener, to unravel the mystery behind a child's prayer that led to instant healing?

_____

_____

_____

_____

What are your thoughts on Dave's statement, "Yet, what you and young Hanna did, I have never seen or experienced before."

_____

_____

_____

_____

What do you think Ben meant when he said:
"The wheat and the tares come together"

_____

_____

_____

_____

What do you think about Ben's description of the
Church? Does his portrayal align with your view
of the Church's role and impact in society?

_____

_____

_____

_____

What was Pastor Dave's response when realizing
that the figure in his nightmare was Jesus, as Ben
read from Revelation?

_____

_____

_____

_____

Do you desire a personal encounter with Jesus, meeting Him face to face?

_____

_____

_____

_____

What do you think motivated Jesus to seek Dave's attention? Why might Jesus choose to appear in a nightmare scenario?

_____

_____

_____

_____

Have you ever sensed a divine warning? What signs did you perceive?

_____

_____

_____

_____

Upon reading chapter 2, what's your perspective on salvation? Do you view it as a singular event or an ongoing journey?

_____

_____

_____

_____

What's your thought on Pastor Dave's repentant prayer, acknowledging his blindness to the Lord's path?

_____

_____

_____

_____

Have you encountered a similar struggle or experience?

_____

_____

_____

_____

What's your thought on Dave's vision of a man with white hair, beard, and fiery eyes, adorned in an ultra-white robe with a golden sash and feet that were like brass?

_____

_____

_____

_____

What emotions would such a vision evoke? Fear? Joy? Dread?

_____

_____

_____

_____

What's your impression of Dave's second vision? How did Lorna and Dave react upon realizing its alignment with Revelation scriptures?

_____

_____

_____

_____

Have you experienced divine visions or communication like this?

_____

_____

_____

_____

What are your opinions on Pastor Dave's repentance, acknowledging errors in his teachings? How do you perceive a pastor's intention to undergo change?

_____

_____

_____

_____

What are your thoughts on fasting? Have you experienced an extended fast, and if so, what was the outcome?

_____

_____

_____

_____

Do you believe dreams have the power to alter someone's life in reality?

_____

_____

_____

_____

3

SOLUTION MODE

Then you will call upon Me and go and
pray to Me, and I will listen to you. And
you will seek Me and find Me, when you
search for Me with all your heart. I will
be found by you, says the LORD,

— JEREMIAH 29:12-14

Have you been on fast recently? Did you encounter any spiritual experience?

_____

_____

_____

_____

What's your perspective on Ben's view of the church as predominantly lukewarm, spiritually sleeping and dead?

_____

_____

_____

_____

What's the significance of being spiritually dead or lukewarm, on our journey with God? In contrast, what does it mean to be spiritually alive?

_____

_____

_____

_____

Have you embarked on a spiritual journey like Dave, going to the mountains to seek a deeper connection with God?

_____

_____

_____

_____

What do you think of Arnold's reaction to Dave's healing? Is healing through prayer a new concept to you, or is it something you consider common-place and expected?

_____

_____

_____

_____

What implications arise from Dave's acknowl-edging treating God like a fairytale?

_____

_____

_____

_____

How did Arnold's shock reflect the significance of Dave's admission?

_____

_____

_____

_____

Does Arnold accurately portray God's nature with his question, "Why would God bother with you as long as you weren't serious about Him?"

_____

_____

_____

_____

What's your thought regarding that God actually "bothers" with someone who hasn't been serious about Him?

_____

_____

_____

_____

Do you encounter skepticism among friends, similar to Arnold's skepticism in the story?

_____

_____

_____

_____

How do you broach up spiritual topics with skeptical friends, fostering open dialogue?

_____

_____

_____

_____

How do you share the gospel message to skeptical friends, ensuring clarity and relevance?

_____

_____

_____

_____

What are your thoughts on Arnold's admission of harassing Dave and joking about God for years?

_____

_____

_____

_____

How do you interpret Dave's decision to stand by Arnold despite his behavior?

_____

_____

_____

_____

Do you find similarities between your friendships and the dynamic between Dave and Arnold?

_____

_____

_____

_____

How significant is Arnold's acknowledgment of, "I and my thinking is the biggest problem for me."? How can Arnold's realization inspire others to address their own challenges?

_____

_____

_____

_____

How do you view your life's journey and the hurdles you've encountered? What do you perceive as the most significant challenge hindering your progress with God?

_____

_____

_____

_____

Moreover, brethren, I declare to you the
gospel which I preached to you, which
also you received and in which you stand,
by which also you are saved, if you hold
fast that word which I preached to you—
unless you believed in vain.

— 1 CORINTHIANS 15:1-2

What do you think about the concept - going to a retreat place while fasting? What do you think of Travis, his usual guests and the drink selection?

_____

_____

_____

_____

What's your opinion of Lorna's audible experience at the cave? Singing a hymn and a choir seems to sing along from the inside of the cave?

_____

_____

_____

_____

Travis' commenting on Dave's dream, "embarrassing" and then explaining, "well, aren't pastors supposed to be awake..." What's your take on this?

_____

_____

_____

_____

Travis sums up Dave's dream, "You haven't been serious about My words. How can you obtain the promises, if you don't have the fear of the Lord? The fear of the Lord, to do what the Lord has told you to do. And at the end, He asks if you are ready?" Is this an adequate summary?

_____

_____

_____

_____

What do you think of Travis's comment: "if you consider the vision with a serious mind, as I sense you do, you might be in for a roller coaster journey which will turn your life around in many respects.

_____

_____

_____

_____

After that Travis says, "When the Lord has taken hold of someone, we see extraordinary things happen, and lives are changed."

Have you or someone you know experienced being taken hold or set apart by the Lord?

_____

_____

_____

_____

Dave said he's not sure he wants change, Travis asks him. "And continue your own way? He awakened you for a reason." What's your take?

_____

_____

_____

_____

When Travis said, "Pastors don't even know their Bible, nor do they preach a Biblical Gospel that converts people." Do you think this statement has roots in reality?

_____

_____

_____

_____

Hearing Travis' opinion about a great portion of the Church and how seeker friendly the pastors and evangelists have become, motivated by budgets and buildings, etc. That shook Dave and Lorna. What's your reaction?

_____

_____

_____

_____

What do you think about the Gospel that offends people? Did it offend you?

_____

_____

_____

_____

Do you feel for Dave when Travis confronts him with a message that hurts?

_____

_____

_____

_____

What do you think of Dave's realization: "No-one seems to have the fear of the Lord"?

_____

_____

_____

_____

What do you think about Dave's statement: "We have been preaching false doctrines"? He admitted for himself, "I have been a false teacher"

_____

_____

_____

_____

Can you imagine the scene when Travis says, "Repent!" to Dave?

_____

_____

_____

_____

What do you think of Travis' description of the greater portion of mankind ending up in hell?

_____

_____

_____

_____

What comes to mind when you hear the expression, "unconverted churchgoers"?

_____

_____

_____

Is repentance, baptism and receiving the Holy Spirit biblical?*

_____

_____

_____

---

* Jesus answered, "Most assuredly, I say to you, unless one is born of water and the Spirit, he cannot enter the kingdom of God. —John 3:5

Did you find something new in this chapter, regarding a Biblical response to the gospel?*

_____

_____

_____

What's your view on: God loves us so "much," implies that He pardons us regardless..."

_____

_____

_____

What do you think of Travis's statement: "A salvation requiring no repentance, no changing of mind and no baptism, as if God was Santa. Many seem to believe this."

_____

_____

_____

---

* Then Peter said to them, "Repent, and let every one of you be baptized in the name of Jesus Christ for the remission of sins; and you shall receive the gift of the Holy Spirit. —Acts 2:38

How would you feel in Dave's place when he realizes he is an unconverted pastor for an unconverted church?

_____

_____

_____

_____

Have you ever asked yourself the question Dave asked himself: "Are we saved?"

_____

_____

_____

_____

"Beat around the bush when we speak about sin" What does this mean to you?

_____

_____

_____

_____

Can you see Lorna's depiction of God's view: "Imagine God, seeing everything. From all mankind He has created, only a tiny group finds their way to Him. Or even want Him in their lives... What is He thinking? HOW does He feel? What can He do?" Can you imagine God's answer to these questions?

_____

_____

_____

_____

How does God's kingdom operate? Travis states that, "...few believers understand how to operate in God's kingdom and His authority. The church doesn't teach about it and believers are tossed around by the world, because they don't know how to tap into the authority we have in Jesus."

_____

_____

_____

_____

Have you heard teachings on how to operate in God's kingdom? What's your opinion?

_____

_____

_____

_____

What do you think of the conversation, quoting bible verses one after the other to prove their points? Have you had a "bible verse fight" like that? Did it end well?

_____

_____

_____

What do you think of Dave's conclusion of their conversation: "It is not like this is all new. It is the way you connect the dots, or the perspective you have. Or it is by removing the clouded lenses we were looking through, that makes this new"

_____

_____

_____

Have you found yourself in a similar situation as Dave described above? Please describe.

_____

_____

_____

Consider Travis' statement regarding God's call: "He is long-suffering and patient waiting on us to respond. It also means, it is up to us who believe and trust Him to spread the Gospel, and that brings me to the other camp of believers called disciples" Who are the disciples today?

_____

_____

_____

What do you think about the fall of Lucifer, who is now Satan, and who is now in charge of the World? Do you agree with this?

_____

_____

_____

Can you explain the difference between Satan's (the World) kingdom and Jesus' kingdom?

_____

_____

_____

_____

"Repentance is to be sorry enough to stop doing what you confess as sin." Does it sound simple or difficult?

_____

_____

_____

What's your take on Travis' questions? "What is your faith? What do you believe? Do you know God well enough to trust Him for your life, salvation and eternity?"

_____

_____

_____

_____

Have you exercised your faith to believe what His word says? Have you, with the fear of the Lord and with the attitude of obedience, done what He has commanded us to do?"

_____

_____

_____

_____

Would you take on Travis' challenge? "You would benefit from reading Acts. And note how Peter and Paul presented the Gospel to Jews and Gentiles. And also note how they signify receiving the Holy Spirit. In Acts you see how the first Church and the Apostles preached and did Church... It could be interesting in relation to how most churches do church today."

_____

_____

_____

_____

What was your conviction prior to reading this chapter, regarding becoming a reborn Christian and a new Creation? Did this chapter challenge your beliefs or theology in any way? Was there any "new" information that made you reconsider your preconceived beliefs?

_____

_____

_____

_____

5

MEETING GOD

My God of mercy shall come to meet me;
God shall let me see my desire on my
enemies.

— PSALM 59:10

Has Dave's "what if" dilemma ever occurred to you? "I was thinking of what would the world look like, if Adam and Eve had children before they fell into sin, or if they had not fallen into sin at all.

"How would the world be? Would we mine for copper, silver, gold and steel? Would we drill for oil? Would we have cars, airplanes, ships and power plants? Could it be that those things are results of the fallen world?"

_____

_____

_____

_____

What do you think of Dave's questions? Are they rhetorical to you too? Or is it still worth contemplating them?

_____

_____

_____

_____

What's your opinion of Lorna's question, "If God would take us out of this world today, where would He bring us? To heaven? If He would take us to heaven, would we pollute it?"

_____

_____

_____

_____

What's your thought regarding Lorna and Dave's repentance prayer? And the physical reaction afterwards? Have you had a similar experience?

_____

_____

_____

_____

Do you practice speaking or praying in tongues? Are you puzzled by "speaking in tongues"?

_____

_____

_____

_____

How do you picture Pentecost? As they contemplate on the issue in the book; how could they baptize 3000 people in one day?

_____

_____

_____

_____

Have you read the Bible with "fresh" eyes, like Dave and Lorna reading Acts? What book was it? What did you learn?

_____

_____

_____

How did you like Dave and Lorna's baptism? Do you agree with the way the baptism was done? What's your take on baptism? Did you baptize in water? Was it similar for you or different? Having read this chapter, has your opinion changed?

_____

_____

_____

_____

What do you think of Lorna's deliverance? Have you prayed for someone to be delivered from demonic activities?

_____

_____

_____

_____

Consider Jim Wallaby and his story. Have you heard a similar story in real life?

_____

_____

_____

_____

What do you think of Jim's prophecy to Dave? Has someone prophesied to you? How was it? What happened?

_____

_____

_____

_____

What do you think of the discussion about demons? What's your opinion? Have you partici-pated in a deliverance prayer before? Have you yourself been set free by someone's prayer?

_____

_____

_____

_____

6

THE MAN GOD USES

Be diligent to present yourself approved
to God, a worker who does not need to be
ashamed, rightly dividing the word of
truth.

— 2 TIMOTHY 2:15

How do you feel about going on a cave exploration? Would you be excited, scared or it is irrelevant to you?

_____

_____

_____

_____

What's your opinion about the message Dave received in the cave?

_____

_____

_____

_____

If you would receive a plan like Dave, how do you think you would handle it?

_____

_____

_____

_____

Have you received directions from God? What was it about?

_____

_____

_____

_____

What did you do about it? How did it turn out?

_____

_____

_____

_____

How does this resonate with you, that Dave and Travis "both sensed that God had knit them together as brothers in Christ"? Have you ever experienced something similar?

_____

_____

_____

_____

What comes to your mind when you hear "disciple training"?

_____

_____

_____

_____

Have you ever faced a task from God bigger than you? How did you handle it? What happened during preparation time? Was it similar to Dave's experience or different?

_____

_____

_____

_____

Have you read the book "The man God uses", by Oswald J. Smith? Do you want to be used by God? What would it be to you; to pay the price, if you would be the man God uses?

_____

_____

_____

If you would ask God the same question Dave did, "What do you think of me, Lord?" What do you think God's answer would be?

_____

_____

_____

What do you think of Dave's prayer experience? (Visiting or seeing Heaven, Hell, spiritually blind people, ignorant.....false spirits, demons....evil is about to crush the people on Earth)

_____

_____

_____

How does this paragraph resonate with you? "God is looking for men and women who will devote themselves to Him and His kingdom. Devote themselves to preach the Gospel and demonstrate the power of God. He is looking for those who will serve without an agenda or twisted truth."

_____

_____

_____

How do you see a fast lasting for a month, like Dave and Lorna is doing?

_____

_____

_____

_____

7

USED BY GOD

Therefore if anyone cleanses himself from the latter, he will be a vessel for honor, sanctified and useful for the Master, prepared for every good work.

— 2 TIMOTHY 2:21

How do you interpret Arnold and Terri's change of mind and awakening interest in God?

_____

_____

_____

_____

Has something caused you, like Arnold to examining his life in light of the Ten commandments? Do you mind elaborate?

_____

_____

_____

_____

When Dave explains the meaning of Jesus' sacrifice, Terri asks, "Why does it have to be so bloody? How come they say God is about Love, when it's so bloody?" What's your thoughts?

_____

_____

_____

_____

What's your take on this Gospel truth, "Jesus paid the price to pardon our sins"?

_____

_____

_____

_____

Consider Dave's description of the process of change, when considering something and consideration changes into realization, it changes from thinking about into knowing. What's your take?

_____

_____

_____

_____

Dave continued by saying that "the knowing" moves from your head to your heart, where you KNOW? Does this resonate with you?

_____

_____

_____

_____

What do you think about Dave lifting Arnold and Terri up in prayer and interceding for their salvation? Are there anyone you can intercede for today?

Ben prayed that God would protect them, not allowing evil to play with their minds, so they would believe. What's your perspective on, "the evil plays with the mind"?

Have you experienced something similar to Terri and Arnold's experience? "They both realized a whole new world had been opened up to them. A world they had heard about, a world that had been distant and unknown to them...

. . .

A world with a new dimension where God existed, where He was in charge of everything"

_____

_____

_____

_____

Thinking of serving God. Consider Arnold's question, "To serve Him in church is one thing. How do we serve Him in business?" Do you think God differs between church and business as two separate places in terms of where He can be served? How would serving Him in those different places differ?

_____

_____

_____

_____

Who is the person of peace - as Dave calls it? "When they trust you, they may listen to your witness of Jesus. That's why Jesus said to his disciples, find a person of peace.

.   .   .

If he doesn't have peace, he won't listen." Do you think he is right? What's your experience with sharing the Gospel?

_____

_____

_____

_____

What's your perspective of money? Is it a goal or a tool for you? Do you agree with Dave, or do you share Arnold's concerns more?

_____

_____

_____

_____

Do you have an opinion of the question Dave asked God, "What is it with us that makes you, almighty God, want us to live?"

_____

_____

_____

_____

What do you think of Travis' saying, "that God was recycling people." And Dave comes to the same conclusion, "It's true! You are really recycling us for Your purpose, for Your kingdom."

_____

_____

_____

_____

8

DISCLOSURE

Therefore do not fear them. For there is nothing covered that will not be revealed, and hidden that will not be known.

— MATTHEW 10:26

What would happen when Dave returns to his own church, healed, baptized and changed? What should he expect?

_____

_____

_____

_____

What do you think about the come-together meeting at Dave's house, did you expect Dave to get in trouble?

_____

_____

_____

_____

How did you receive Dave's explanation about what happened to them?

_____

_____

_____

_____

How would you describe John's reaction? Do you agree or disagree with him saying, "Nobody does what you say. To my knowledge, there is no church or minister that does any of these things. There is no tradition nor practice of what you say. If we start practicing these things, wouldn't that break the mold of the church? Wouldn't it destroy the church we know?"

_____

_____

_____

_____

What's your opinion of Dave's question, "The church we know ... we need to ask ourselves, is the church we know the church of Jesus Christ?"

_____

_____

_____

_____

Jesus said: "heal the sick, cast out demons"? Is it the normal Christian life to you? Do you practice this? What about making disciples as Jesus told us to do?

_____

_____

_____

_____

Do you think John is right when he says: "Nobody does that today"? Have you met anybody practicing this?

_____

_____

_____

_____

Did you hear about the expression, the Peter package, "Repent! Believe! Baptize! Receive!". Is this question, "Does anyone preach this message today?", legit?

_____

_____

_____

_____

Do you believe Dave is right when saying, "By demonstrating the power of God's kingdom, they will realize who God is"? Does it really happen this way?

_____

_____

_____

_____

What do you think is the answer to Harry's question: "Sir, how can we become empty.....vessels?"

_____

_____

_____

_____

If you grew up in a traditional church how would you handle Dave's explanation of being born again?

_____

_____

_____

_____

If you were baptized as a baby, what's your perspective on Dave's questions, "When they baptized you, did you repent? Did you believe? Did you receive the Holy Spirit?"

_____

_____

_____

_____

Is Dave right asking this: "What are the chances of being reborn, if you miss three of four Biblical requirements?"

_____

_____

_____

Have you experienced like John did, when hearing a new revelation about God's truth, being stirred up and not being able to sleep?

_____

_____

_____

Consider what John said to Dave, "Well, it is hard to realize the possibility of being on the wrong side of salvation despite believing to be safe. I need advice on salvation." How would you advise an "old Christian" in this situation?

_____

_____

_____

_____

Think of Oswald J. Smith's observation of the church, 'The line of demarcation has been so completely broken down, that churches, where revival once flourished, whose spiritual life was at one time deep and strong, are today mere social centers over which God has long ago written the word — Ichabod — the glory has departed.'

Would you agree or disagree with Oswald?

_____

_____

_____

_____

9

CALLED TO SERVICE

Is anyone among you sick? Let him call
for the elders of the church, and let them
pray over him, anointing him with oil in
the name of the Lord. And the prayer of
faith will save the sick, and the Lord will
raise him up.

— JAMES 5:14-15

Do you know what a Chaplain or a priest does in a hospital when patients call for them? Have you ever witnessed something like that? Do you think Dave followed the accepted protocol?

_____

_____

_____

Have you been present when a person was about to die? How was it? How did you handle the situation? Does it still affect you?

_____

_____

_____

Do you think abortion is a sin? How big of a sin? Do you think, if you abort a child, will God punish you? Can someone have children after abortion?

_____

_____

_____

_____

What's your impression of a woman confessing a sin she committed 20-30 years ago? Why would she wait so long, what do you think? Have you been in a similar situation, not confessing a sin for a long time?

_____

_____

_____

_____

What's your take on whether God forgives all our sins or there is something He can not forgive?

_____

_____

_____

_____

Do you believe it is normal or usual that people's secrets come to the surface only before their death (deathbed confessions), like the woman at the hospital saying, "fear of dying with my sin became greater than my fear of people knowing about it"

If we look at sin and our condition in front of God and His judgment, are you ready to face it?

_____

_____

_____

_____

Do you think Dave's description of the devil is accurate? "Our enemy, the devil will do anything possible for us to hold onto our secrets, to shy us away from confession. He knows that if we confess, God is faithful to forgive." Does he work as described? Do you have first hand experience?

_____

_____

_____

How is your experience with God, as a forgiving Lord or rather angry at sin?

_____

_____

_____

Was Dave right describing God this way: "If we trust God, He will deliver us. But you must trust Him enough to confess to Him."

_____

_____

_____

What do you think of the council's meeting? Did you expect that the council members would oppose change, either fully or partly? Who would you likely side with? Do you like changes of routine or are you absolutely against them?

_____

_____

_____

10
SUNDAY MORNING SERVICE

... do not worry beforehand, or premeditate what you will speak. But whatever is given you in that hour, speak that; for it is not you who speak, but the Holy Spirit.

— MARK 13:11B

Have you been under spiritual attack, as Dave was before preaching the Sunday service message? What did you face after a sleepless night? How was your message received?

_____

_____

_____

_____

Have you ever prayed for yourself or somebody else to be delivered from demonic activities?

_____

_____

_____

_____

How do you like Babette's story told in church by the atheist Dr. Longworth?

_____

_____

_____

_____

What do you think happened inside Babette after talking to Dave?

_____

_____

_____

_____

What do you think of what the atheist doctor witnessed in his hospital?

_____

_____

_____

_____

If you were in his shoes, how would you react to Babette's healing?

_____

_____

_____

_____

If you were a nurse at the hospital, how would you handle the situation of filling up the bathtub for a dying cancer patient?

_____

_____

_____

_____

Have you seen someone being so sick that the doctors gave up on them, just to see them become perfectly well? How did that happen?

_____

_____

_____

What's your impression of the church service at Dave's church? What do you think would happen in the church after hearing such strong testimonies, and the powerful gospel pre-sentation?

_____

_____

_____

_____

Have you ever heard, or even preached a sermon like Dave's, quoting Jonathan Edwards, "that because of our sin we deserve hell" and "Your wickedness makes you as heavy as lead and to tend downwards with great weight and pressure towards hell"?

Have you felt the weight of your sins? Do you see the redemption Dave describes? "God knows what we need for Him to elevate us out of the valley of misery, if we are willing. God knows the price tag to redeem us. Blood money! And also knows that our blood wouldn't do... His Son, after creating us, took on himself to pay the penalty for our redemption. He did that to create an escape route for us to live the life he created us for."

What was your salvation experience with God? What was God's way to you?

_____

_____

_____

_____

Consider the following statements: "He was dead for three days, and He rose again by the power of God." "That resurrection is our anchor and hope, our reason to trust in God for our salvation." What feeling rises up in you reading these words?

_____

_____

_____

_____

What are your answers to Dave questions in his sermon, "Do you want to meet an angry God for judgment? An angry God who will show you everything you have done? An angry God who will ask you why did you not heed His call to repent? Who will ask you why you didn't believe in

His Son Jesus Christ? Why didn't you do what Jesus said: be baptized in water and receive his Holy Spirit? Why?"

Is God only angry? No, he isn't. God is a kind, devoted Father to His dear children, who loves them. But, He's also a consuming fire. What do you think?

While reading, did you examine yourself? Are you a child of God? Have you repented? Have you confessed your sins to God? Have you experienced recreation, reborn in water and Spirit? Does the Holy Spirit dwell in you? Do you have a relationship with Jesus?

11
AFTERMATH

Jesus answered and said to him, "If anyone loves Me, he will keep My word; and My Father will love him, and We will come to him and make Our home with him.

— JOHN 14:23

How would it mean to you, if saw a dear childhood friend come to Jesus?

_____

_____

_____

_____

What if she or he asks you to baptize them? How would you react? For whom do you pray for, to get saved?

_____

_____

_____

What could happen if all the pastors and congregations in town catch the fire of the Holy Spirit and come alive, like Dave thought of his town and work together with pastors from different denominators?

_____

_____

_____

Do you think it possible that all the pastors would leave their doctrines and doctrinal differences behind and just follow the Bible?

_____

_____

_____

_____

What about your town, could it possibly happen there? Remember Dave's words, "God was God for all. Jesus died the same death for all."

_____

_____

_____

Consider Dave's statement, "He didn't think God intended to separate the church into factions." Do you think Dave is right? Why then, do we have so many denominations?

_____

_____

_____

What about Reggie's statement, "We have not obeyed His commandments any of us." Is Reggie right? Could this realization cause a change? Or at least make them seek and search for the truth?

_____

_____

_____

What is the difference between unconverted church goers and church shoppers?

_____

_____

_____

_____

Why do you think the hospital Chaplain came to Dave's church? What was the doctor's goal in inviting the Chaplain to church?

_____

_____

_____

_____

What's your thought on the pastor's Bible study, discussing miracles as means to convince people? Do you agree or disagree with Ben? "Don't think a miracle would change them. Some would change, perhaps. I have seen people walking with great difficulty. Once healed, they have been running away as fast as their healed legs would carry them."

_____

_____

_____

_____

"People don't seem to seek God before they hit rock bottom in their life." Do you agree with this statement? Or do you have a different experience?

_____

_____

_____

_____

What do you think about persecution, will it produce hard-core believers? How many would leave the church, when or if the Church of Christ is persecuted?

_____

_____

_____

_____

What is your take of Jesus' words? "Any branch not bearing fruit, will be cut off and burned."* What does it mean to be cut off?

_____

_____

_____

Have you considered the parable of the sower, wondering which soil you are? Which one do you think?

_____

_____

_____

_____

* John 15.2

What would you do or tell a person, to move them from being one type of soil to the next? Or to make their heart soil type four eventually?

_____

_____

_____

_____

What do you think of Ruth's son and his story?

_____

_____

_____

_____

Have you met young men, full of bitterness and hatred, playing war games all the time?

_____

_____

_____

_____

12

DISCIPLESHIP

After these things the Lord appointed seventy others also, and sent them two by two before His face into every city and place where He Himself was about to go.

— LUKE 10:1

Who or what, in your opinion, is a disciple? Do you see them around?

_____

_____

_____

_____

Did your definition of a disciple change in your mind while reading this chapter?

_____

_____

_____

_____

Have you experienced that the demons were subject to you, like the seventy returning to Jesus in the Luke 10 story? "The seventy returned with joy saying: "Lord, even the demons are subject to us in Your name."

_____

_____

_____

_____

Can you relate to this statement, ".... many things that God sees as sin, have become accepted and common in our society." Can you list some things, which you think is sin but accepted by society?

_____

_____

_____

_____

Do you think the following statement is true of today's believers and churches? "Even if they preach the Gospel and declare the commandments, most of them sit in the pews and then go home, doing nothing."

_____

_____

_____

What about the churches in your town?

_____

_____

_____

Do you think Ben is right saying this, "Believers sit in church waiting. The Word says: Go! Preach! Heal! They are not doing what Jesus told them to do."?

_____

_____

_____

_____

What do you think about the harvest? Is it ready?

_____

_____

_____

_____

Who should be working in the field for the harvest?

_____

_____

_____

_____

Do you think Ben is right saying, "The harvest is always ready, but believers are not doers. Believers need to become active doers of God's will. Doers who get out, meet the people where the people are"? What's your opinion?

_____

_____

_____

_____

Where is your harvest field? How do you do the harvest?

_____

_____

_____

_____

Is it true or not true: "Those who try to follow the commands of Jesus are seen as the odd and tricky ones."?

_____

_____

_____

Consider the statement: "...there is a cost in doing what Jesus called us to do."* Do you believe it's true?

If so, what would the cost be for you?

_____

_____

_____

_____

Do you have someone around you to ask for prayer to be healed?

_____

_____

_____

_____

Do you have a sickness or diseases to prayed for? Go to the https://map.thelastreformation.com and find someone near you to connect with.

❧

---

* Mt 16. 24-25; Luke 9.25-26

Have you seen someone get healed in front of your eyes?

Have you ever gone on the streets to pray for people?

What happened?

_____

_____

_____

_____

Have you seen healing testimonies on YouTube? You can watch some here:

https://thelastreformation.com/movies/the-beginning

What do you think of them? Does it stir up faith in you?

_____

_____

_____

_____

13
THE PROPHET

Now I saw when the Lamb opened one
of the seals; and I heard one of the four
living creatures saying with a voice like
thunder, "Come and see."

— REVELATION 6:1

What do you think a prophet looks like today?
Have you met one?

_____

_____

_____

_____

What is prophecy? Telling the future or warning
about judgment like in the Old Testament or
something else?*

_____

_____

_____

What do you think, where are we now in the biblical timeline?

_____

_____

_____

_____

_____

* Read 1 Cor. ch. 12 and ch. 14 for biblical Prophecy

Is the prophet correct with his suggestions? If yes, why? If not, why?

_____

_____

_____

_____

Do you follow the news? Is it true that, "the same news often are on all channels at the same time, even with the exact same wording"?

_____

_____

_____

_____

Do you think the media shapes people's opinion big time?

_____

_____

_____

_____

Do you think there are world leaders preparing to take over and that the New World Order and a One World Government will come to pass?

Could this be a real conspiracy or do you see it as purely as a fictional theory?

_____

_____

_____

_____

Could this happen in reality; "Evil will be on display to such a degree that even the most deeply slumbering believer will wake up and cry out to God."?

_____

_____

_____

_____

If calamities like "Earthquakes, volcanos, and tsunamis, would hit the nation," how would that affect the nation?

· · ·

Would you see such events as warning and harbingers of what to come if they won't wake up? Or would you see it as purely nature events without any connection to God and His people?

_____

_____

_____

If a scenario as described would come to pass, what would you do in respect of the statement, "God needs His people to stand up and fight along with Him"?

_____

_____

_____

You have probably heard of conspiracy theories before? What was it? What makes something a conspiracy theory?

_____

_____

_____

_____

"God needs His church to wake up, to stand with Him and fight with Him. To wake up the church, He will allow the enemy to move ahead with their plans... The longer it takes for the Church to wake up and take its place, the darker it will become. When God's people will cry out in sustained cry, He will move."

Do you think this could be a prophecy also in the real world, for today or near future? If yes, why? If not, why?

_____

_____

_____

_____

How would you feel if your were in Dave's place when the prophet tells him:

"In that dark hour, you, Pastor, will speak to the people, and broadcast to the nation. That is the moment God is preparing you for.

_____

_____

_____

_____

Can you imagine a situation where the Prophet's words would happen in real life, that God's people, on a big scale or nationwide, would humble themselves, confess their own sins and the nation's sins too?

_____

_____

_____

_____

How do you handle sudden bad news? Consider Dave when hearing his wife was shot and other leaders at his church. What would your possible reaction be?

_____

_____

_____

_____

14

DAVE MEETS LORNA

"Hear now My words:
If there is a prophet among you,
I, the LORD, make Myself known to him
in a vision; I speak to him in a dream.

— NUMBERS 12:6

How did you handle the fact that Dave's wife Lorna died?

_____

_____

_____

_____

Have you experienced grief? How was it? How long did it take to overcome it?

_____

_____

_____

_____

Have you seen a family without a mum? How did that family function?

_____

_____

_____

_____

How do you think Pastor Dave's life will continue forward?

This question may take a whole book to answer, and people have asked:

What happened to the murderer?

How did the church handle the situation?

What did they do?

What about the funeral?

Who performed the Sermon?

How did the remnant react to the tragic event?

Perhaps these questions will be answered one day...

ACKNOWLEDGMENT

The Last Reformation (TLR) is a movement where people from many different churches and denominations find teaching and discipleship. It was started by a young Danish man, Torben Sondergaard, who, after searching for more with God, began a ministry where the original Church in the Acts is central.

As he began his ministry, he experienced profound healings and miracles, and made headlines.

❧

English Pastor and Bible teacher, David Pawson, originally a Methodist pastor, became baptized as an adult and became a Baptist minister. He later was baptized in the Holy Spirit and has been teaching the Bible around the world. In New Zealand he was named Mr. Peacock, as Travis mentions.

Pawson died 2020 at 90 years of age, and has left behind a great legacy of video teachings on YouTube.

My favorites lessons of his are his sermon, "True God - True Gospel," and his 6 – part series on "How to become a Christian."

Further there is a 13 – part "In Depth Interview." If you are interested, that gives a very good picture of who David Pawson was at his legacy website.

The teaching of David Pawson and the practical discipling movement, The Last Reformation, have contributed greatly to how we go about our everyday Christian life, and have influenced the writing of this book.

ABOUT THE AUTHOR

I grew up in a secular home in Norway, where church mattered at Christmas, weddings, baby baptisms and funerals. Becoming a believer at the age of 40 in 2000, that changed, I baptized in South Africa.

Back in Europe, and in 2016 we came in contact with a movement called "The Last Reformation" (TLR), and an English Pastor teacher David Pawson.

David Pawson's teaching and workshops with practical training with TLR, a small group of us began ministering, walking the streets of Budapest, Europe.

You can find me on http://x.com/JanFSolvberg.

Please review this book!

★★★★★

Reviews help authors more than you might think. If you enjoyed *God's Remnant - When God,* please consider leaving a review on Amazon. A couple of sentences to say how you found the book. It would be greatly appreciated, because it helps us keep going, creating more for you to read.

★★★★★

Please, follow the link, God's Remnant – When God... Workbook

Or, scan the code below to review

Review the book